The Library of Healthy Living

Staying Healthy:

Alice B. McGinty

The Rosen Publishing Group's
PowerKids Press™
New York

Published in 1997 by The Rosen Publishing Group, Inc.
29 East 21st Street, New York, NY 10010

First Edition

Book Design: Kim Sonsky

Photo Illustrations: Cover and all photo illustrations by Seth Dinnerman.

McGinty, Alice B.
      Staying healthy: Sleep and rest / Alice B. McGinty.
         p.   cm. (The library of healthy living)
      Summary: Describes the stages of sleep, discusses what happens when we sleep and why we
   need sleep.
      ISBN 0-8239-5138-3
      1. Sleep—Juvenile literature. [1. Sleep.] I. Title. II. Series.
   QP425.M394 1997
   613.7'9—dc21   96-37359
                                                                                                CIP
                                                                                                 AC

Manufactured in the United States of America

Contents

Everybody Needs Rest

You work hard every day. You move, think, and listen. You use your eyes, your muscles, and your brain. At night, your eyes feel heavy. You're all out of energy. Your body is telling

4

you it needs to rest.

People need sleep.

Some people sleep during the day. Some sleep at night. Some nap. Everybody sleeps!

You spend a lot of time sleeping. Why do you need sleep? What goes on inside your body when you sleep?

Why You Need Sleep

Why do you need to spend so much time sleeping? Your body uses the time during sleep to do important things.

While you sleep:
- ☺ You grow.
- ☺ Your body fights off germs that can make you sick.

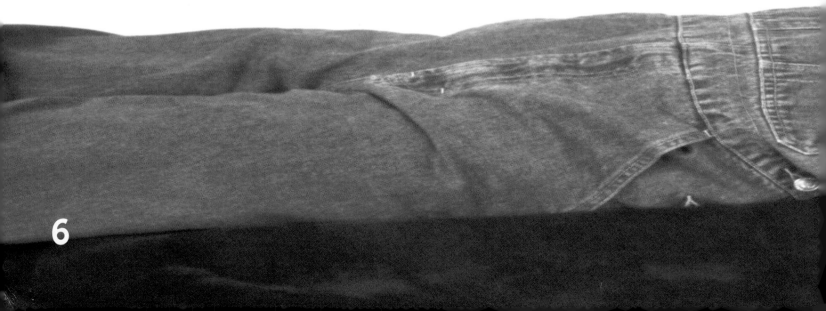

☺ Some parts of your body rest, such as your muscles and eyes.

☺ You store up enough energy to work and play for another day.

What Happens When You Sleep?

Many other things go on inside your body while you sleep. Your heartbeat changes. Your breathing changes. Sometimes you wiggle or turn over.

As you sleep, your heartbeat does not stay the same. Sometimes it slows down. Sometimes it beats faster. Your breathing and your movements go through changes too.

Scientists who study sleep know that the changes in your body happen in steps, called **stages** (STAY-jez).

The Sleep Cycle

When you sleep, your body goes through five stages. The first stage of sleep is called light sleep. Your muscles **relax** (ree-LAX). Your heartbeat slows. You breathe evenly.

The second stage of sleep is a little bit heavier. It lasts between five and fifteen minutes. The third stage, in which you spend the least amount of time, is heavier still.

The fourth stage is the

10

deepest stage of sleep. You may stay in stage four sleep for as long as 20 to 40 minutes. The last stage of sleep is called **REM sleep** (REM SLEEP).

Together, these stages are called the **sleep cycle** (SLEEP SY-kul). You go through the sleep cycle several times each night.

◄ *Snoring can happen at any stage of sleep!*

REM Sleep

The last stage of sleep is REM sleep. REM stands for Rapid Eye Movement. You spend between 90 and 120 minutes of sleep per night in REM sleep.

You dream during REM sleep. Your eyes move underneath your closed eyelids to "see" your dream.

During dreams, people you know and things you have seen or heard come together in funny ways. Dreams can be nice or scary. Scary dreams are called **nightmares** (NYT-mayrz).

Everyone has dreams, although some people may not remember them.

In REM sleep, your heartbeat and breathing are sometimes fast and sometimes slow.

◄ *Some nightmares are about scary monsters.*
Others may be about scary situations.

What Are Dreams?

What are dreams? Nobody really knows. People have many different ideas about why we dream.

Dreaming happens in your brain. While you are awake, your brain records information from your **senses** (SEN-sez)—what you see, hear, touch, taste, and smell. Your brain **interprets** (in-TER-prets) the information that the senses send. That information is turned into thoughts.

Many scientists believe that your brain gets so much information, you can't go through all of it during the day. They think dreams happen when your brain sorts through the information at night.

Sometimes people dream about normal, everyday things. Other times they dream about things that don't seem to make any sense at all. ▶

How Much Sleep?

The younger you are, the more sleep you need. Babies sleep almost all the time. Their bodies and minds grow quickly, so they need extra rest. Their brains sort through lots of information about the new world around them.

Toddlers sleep all night and nap each day. School-aged children sleep about ten to twelve hours each night. Adults usually sleep for seven or eight hours each night. Each person needs a different amount of sleep. Some people need sleep more than others. When you get enough sleep, your mind and body feel rested. You also have more energy.

17

When You Don't Get Enough Sleep

What happens when you *don't* get enough sleep?

You probably feel grouchy. Little things make you angry or upset. Your body has less energy. You get tired quickly. You may not feel like doing anything. It is hard to pay attention at school or follow the words in a book. You may make mistakes or forget things. Your eyelids feel heavy.

Have you ever felt this way? Your body is telling you that it needs rest.

Sleeping Problems

Sometimes it's hard to fall asleep or stay asleep. If you are excited or worried, your mind may be too busy to fall asleep. This happens to everyone at some time. Luckily, you can recover from a bad night of sleep by sleeping well the next night.

Not being able to sleep for many nights in a row is called **insomnia** (in-SOM-nee-uh). If this happens to you, tell your parents or your doctor. They can help you find ways to get the sleep you need.

Some people talk or walk in their sleep. These things are usually harmless. Most of the time, people don't even remember doing them. And sleepwalking usually stops when a person gets older.

Being a Good Sleeper

You can help make your body healthy and strong by being a good sleeper. Here is what you can do.

Rest during the day. Have quiet time or take a nap. Go to bed at about the same time each night. Do quiet things before bed, such as reading a book or listening to stories. Sleep in a dark, quiet place so your eyes and ears can relax. Get plenty of sleep.

Rest your body for a strong, healthy you!

Glossary

insomnia (in-SOM nee-uh) Not being able to sleep.

interpret (in-TER-pret) To change from one kind of information to another.

nightmare (NYT-mayr) Scary dream.

relax (ree-LAX) To loosen up.

REM sleep (REM SLEEP) The last stage of the sleep. cycle. REM stands for Rapid Eye Movement.

senses (SEN-sez) The things (sight, hearing, smell, taste, and touch) that give you information about the world around you.

sleep cycle (SLEEP SY-kul) The five stages of sleep.

stages (STAY-jez) The steps or parts of sleep.

Index